GW00721991

Jeannie McDougall's
HAGGIS
WHISKY
PORRIDGE
TARTAN
BAGPIPES
and all that!

"Haggis, Whisky, Porridge, Tartan, Bagpipes and all that".
Published by Lang Syne Publishers Ltd., 45 Finnieston Street, Glasgow G3 8JU.
Printed by Dave Barr Print, 45 Finnieston Street, Glasgow G3 8JU.

© LANG SYNE PUBLISHERS LTD. 1982.
First published April 1, 1982. Reprinted 1994

ISBN N0. 0 946264 65 1

Heatherbell Cottage,
Dramlochy,
Kilt-in-the-Heather,
Caledonia.

Friday, April 1.

Dear Reader,

Thank you very much indeed for kindly picking up a copy of my book.

As I sit by the window, watching the stream run by the bottom of the garden, pen in one hand and a glass of something substantial to keep out the night chill in the other, I am thinking of my childhood days.

Then the Lady of this house was my mother -- a determined, strict yet kind and gentle soul. Her principal preoccupations were that we ate up all our porridge before going to school in the morning, did our homework before tea, helped milk the cows and attended church twice on Sundays.

Despite our formal upbringing we children -- I've four brothers and two sisters -- were very, very happy. I remember the simple things best ... like skipping over the stepping stones of the stream on the way to school; coming home on a cold winter's day to a plate of home made Scotch broth and old fashioned bannocks with strong tea; playing peever or chap-door-run on the village houses ... country dancing in the parish hall.

A shepherd marched over the hills each evening playing the bagpipes -- he was our nearest neighbour and lived four miles away.

Sadly these days are long gone. A motorway now runs past the backdoor and jumbo jets terrify the heatherbells to death as they zoom over our roof after taking off from the new airport nearby.

However such problems are minor when we consider what is happening to other great Scottish institutions like the bagpipe tree and the minmac, the "wee cow" that gave generations of Scots condensed milk, -- both are almost extinct.

Smugglers and the excisemen are causing such havoc with our whisky that the high prices are driving us to drink even more.

On top of that the Japs have invented powdered whisky and butchers are making artificial haggis because folk are too idle to go out on to the moors and shoot the blooming birds themselves.

I ask you: where will it all end?

That's why I've set down my thoughts in this book. If it achieves nothing more it will at least clear up some of the daft misconceptions a lot of folk have about haggis, whisky, porridge, tartan, bagpipes and all that!

And a happy April Fool's Day to you all.

Yours for Caledonia,
Jeannie McDougall

HAGGIS-FROM THE SCOTS "LOVHAGIBIRCALEDIS — ALL THE BEST BIRDS ARE IN CALEDONIA"

Odd though it may seem there are actually people around who think that real haggis is manufactured by butchers ... tartan is woven in mills ... whisky flows from places called distilleries ... bagpipes are made by craftsmen ... and porridge comes from an oat plant.

Such ignorant souls are also convinced that Nessie, our beloved monster whose home is in the depths of Loch Ness, is an invention of the tourist trade designed to attract visitors.

They will eat hens eggs for breakfast and buy their children chocolate eggs at Easter. But try having a serious discussion about the problems of thieves who pinch sporrans eggs for resale on the black market and they will laugh in your face.

Its high time the record was set straight.

For a start let's take the haggis.

I find it disgraceful that certain butchers should make haggis in the rear of their shops and pass it off to unsuspecting shoppers as the real thing.

The wonders of science and, in fairness, a certain amount of skill permits them to give us a product which tastes just like freshly caught haggis. Often it can be a few pence cheaper as well.

My palate is fortunately such that I can always spot the fake food when it is served up to me.

Recently I became a legend in my own lunchtime after being presented with such a plateful in a Glasgow hotel.

Without hesitation I rose from my table marched to the kitchen and dispensed the offensive nosh over the chef's head.

Later, when asked to explain my actions in court, I told the magistrate in no uncertain terms that the day had come for all right thinking folk to rise up and campaign against the imitation haggis.

Unfortunately he replied that the only campaign which interested him was the compulsory restoration of the quarter gill in all hostelries north of Berwick upon Tweed.

I was fined £50.

THE HAGGIS SHOOT-OUTS

The development of this instant gunge has grown up in recent years because fewer folk are willing to tramp the moors in search of the haggis which is found mainly in Perthshire and Argyll.

For centuries dinner tables all over Scotland have been graced with the bird. It can be legally shot or netted between August 12 and Christmas Eve each year.

Oddly enough all haggis babies are born on April 1 and by August they've grown to their full weight of ten pounds.

The haggis — from the ancient Scots lovhagibircaledis: all the best birds are in Caledonia — lives in a nest which is shaped rather like a giant beehive.

It is not uncommon for several 'families' to live under the one roof and the population of each nest is usually around 25.

They have tiny wings which enable them to fly but not for more than a few hundred yards at a time.

The haggis is happiest just bouncing along the ground but must be on constant guard against humans who come hunting with net in one hand and gun in the other.

Although the sport of haggis-baiting is in decline I and a few dedicated others are still willing to spend long weary hours searching for this rare delicacy.

Idleness is of course one factor why many folks don't bother going out to catch their dinner.

Another -- and I have to say much more sinister -- reason is the mushrooming of pressure groups which are campaigning for a total ban on all netting and shooting.

The AASH campaign -- Action Against Haggis Shooting -- and the HOOTS-H brigade -- Hands Off Our Timid Shy Haggis -- are the most active protestors.

Recently a haggis hunt in Perthshire turned into a full scale riot when battles broke out between rival factions.

Hunters and opponents beat the living daylights out of one another.

The hunted haggis responded by rising into the air and dispensing the contents of their bowels directly onto the haggis-stalker hatted folk below.

The haggis shooting season in full swing.

Nobody carrying a gun or net was sacrosanct.

And when I tell you that the bowels of a haggis are 10 times bigger than those of a seagull I'm pretty sure that you will have a clear picture of the ensuing scenes of chaos.

"SCOTCH AND WRY!" THEY CRIED

More trouble at another haggis hunt in Argyll received national press and television coverage.

"80 INJURED 126 ARRESTED IN HAGGIS VIOLENCE" read one headline.

The paper's man on the spot reported:--

"A full scale riot broke out in Argyll yesterday when angry haggis hunters and conservationists clashed near Oban.

Protestors from AASH and HOOTS-H disrupted the hunt when it was just five minutes under way by blowing anti-haggis horns and crying: Jeely Piece! Jeely Piece! Scotch and Wry! Scotch and Wry!"

An AASH spokesman explained that the cry would make the animals scurry immediately to secret underground bunkers as the mere mention of jam sandwiches and whisky with ginger ale terrifies them.

"Members of the Hunt, under the command of Lord Bridie, immediately hit back by shouting: 'Irn Bru! Irn Bru!' and playing tapes of Sir Harry Lauder songs.

"The passion of the haggis for Irn Bru, Scotland's other national drink, and Sir Harry Lauder songs is of course well known but on this occasion the haggis did not rise to the bait.

"Furious huntsmen then charged at the saboteurs and bloody fighting broke out.

"Two landrovers were set on fire and 563 bottles of malt whisky which had been brought along for after-hunt drinks were smashed.

"More than 80 people were injured, five seriously, and police who arrived on the scene within minutes made 126 arrests."

Meanwhile our parliamentary correspondent writes, today a group of furious Scots MPs are to table a Commons motion calling on the Prime Minister to outlaw haggis hunting.

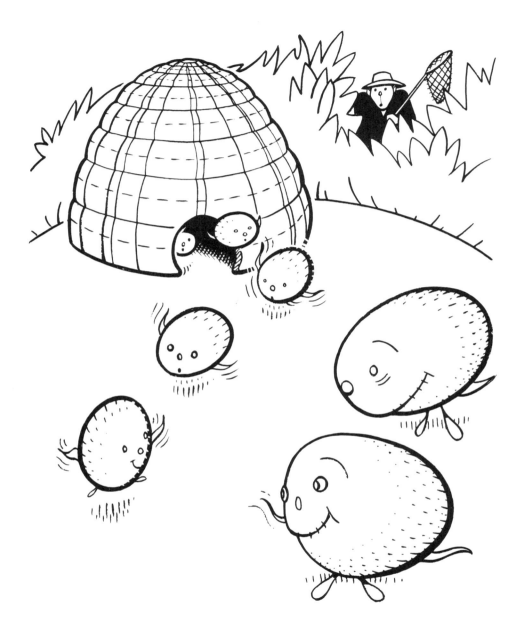

Baby Haggis can't fly. They just flutter around the nest. But they must watch out for cunning folk who try and net them. Baby haggis is a rare delicacy and very popular on the black market. It cannot legally be sold openly.

'This evil vile and cruel sport must be stopped and stopped quickly,' said Sir John Rentaquote, the honourable member for Haggisville.

'For centuries this defenceless wee bird has been taken from his home and killed for people's dinner tables.

'As society has supposedly become more civilised since hunting was made legal in 1314 I call on all right thinking people to rise up and say: 'Enough is enough! Let us eat roast beef and Yorkshire pudding instead!'

"Angry Tory MPs however plan an amendment saying that haggis hunting should be allowed to continue.

"They point out that any changes in the existing legislation could be disastrous for the Scottish economy as well as a below the belt hit at haggis gourmets.

"The Liberals and Scottish Nationalists will hold the balance in this crucial situation but at Westminster last night whips refused to say how their MPs would be voting."

As you can imagine I spent a sleepless night wondering how things would go but fortunately for me and others who love to eat real haggis the minority parties sided with the Government and thus a crisis was averted.

HAGGIS HUNTS: NO BAN and CARRY ON HUNTING ran the headlines next day.

Phew! What a relief!

Doune Castle

S. Young 85.

MR. & MRS. JAMES McKELVEY
10, ELM COURT
DOUNE
PERTHSHIRE
FK16 6JG
TEL: 0786 841049

16/5/94

Dear Jenny,

Here is a little
book which I hope you will
enjoy, and then perhaps employ
as a reliable manual to
instruct the pupils at the
school, all thirsting for
knowledge of Haggis and
other things Scottish.

Anyway, I send it to you
now, with my best wishes
and in appreciation of all

that you do for the Bessingtatch branch of the family.

It was a great pleasure meeting you, and Terry.

Yours affectionately

"Uncle" Jimmie

A haggis football match.

WHY THEY SWIM TO TOBERMORY

Although the lifetime of a haggis is short they really do enjoy themselves between April and August or until such times as the hunter's net can be dodged no more!

The Perthshire haggis is light brown in colour with pink eyes and a cheeky smile.

Babies are bottle fed on Irn Bru for the first week and they can talk their language of Hagaelic fluently from the end of the second week. In week three they are moved on to solids like oatcakes, black bun and carrots.

All this continues to be washed down by Irn Bru -- the haggis have exclusive use of underwater streams which flow red with this magnificent liquid -- and it is interesting to note that the average adult haggis gets through three to four pints a day of the stuff.

It is this penchant for Irn Bru which is thought to give the haggis its unique flavour as far as human consumption is concerned.

The haggis has three main forms of defence when hunted.

1. A quick leap into the air and discharge of its enormous bowel content as mentioned earlier.

2. Superb hearing. A haggis perched on Gleneagles Hotel roof can hear a pipe band playing in Perth.

3. Razor sharp needles on the back which have caused many a careless hunter to turn and flee with blood pouring from hand or face.

Their favourite pastime is football. The haggis use a newly laid sporrans egg which they hard boil and think nothing of playing a game for as much as five hours.

The Argyllshire haggis is similar in appearance with a slightly darker skin and blue eyes.

They tend to be more shy.

Oddly enough when an Argyll haggis couple decide to mate the prospective mother and father make their way to the coast near Oban and swim up the Sound of Mull to Tobermory.

On this peaceful island the young are conceived and the pair then head back to Argyll in time for the birth on April 1.

The haggis piped in for Burns Supper.

It is quite a sight to stand on the deck of a Caledonian MacBrayne steamer and watch the young lovers swim into the distance.

Natural haggis must be kept for a month after being caught so that the meat can fully mature. It is best placed in a saucepan of condensed milk and Irn Bru (which is now available in bottles due to the inaccessability of bru streams to humans) and covered for a month.

The haggis must be eaten however no more than one month and one day after capture.

This is why those shot on the last day of the season --December 24 -- have pride of place at Burns Suppers held all over the world on the following January 25.

Its a great sight to see the haggis piped in and no wonder our national bard Rabbie Burns was moved to write:

Fair fa' your honest sonsie face,
Great Chieftan o' the Puddin-race,
Aboon them a' ye tak your place
Paich, tripe or thairm,
Weel are ye wordy of a grace
As lang's my arm.

THE DRAMBUSTERS!

Whisky -- the water of life -- is Scotland's national drink by tradition. For centuries we have partaken of a refreshment in the form of a dram to make the journey along life's highway a more pleasant one.

Served as a nip in Edinburgh and a half in Glasgow this wee goldie in the glass warms the heart and lightens the brain.

But as we down drams in the company of good friends and family it is all too easy to forget the men who risk their lives to bring us our favourite tipple.

Day and night all year round brave fellows challenge nature at its rawest and drill for our whisky in the stormy waters of the North Sea.

Until a decade ago all whisky production was from fields on land. But as these supplies became exhausted new frontiers had to be explored.

Revolutionary survey techniques were used to drill holes in the seabed in search of drams.

The first major field was discovered in 400 feet of water some 100 miles off Aberdeen in 1970. Production began in 1973.

Around 500,000 gallons a day is piped ashore from here for refining at mainland distilleries.

Meanwhile eight other fields have been developed and these bring in whisky which is worth millions of pounds on the international market.

Aberdeen has benefited enormously from the spin off and has become Britain's drams capital.

Many folk have become millionaires by servicing this booming new offshore enterprise through the provision of catering facilities, specialist clothing, high speed transport and so on.

SMUGGLERS ON THE SEABED

Unfortunately a more sinister trade has also grown up -- smuggling. In days gone by whisky smugglers were a common part of the scene particularly in the Highlands.

Scots folk were violently opposed to the high taxes slapped on their liquid gold by successive Governments so the smuggler was treated as something of a local hero and the exciseman received little assistance in attempts to bring him to justice.

Today however it is organised crime like the Mafia who are behind much of the illicit whisky operations. They're literally syphoning off a fortune by tampering with underwater pipes on the seabed.

In a recent court case 10 men were arrested after months of painstaking work by detectives in an operation codenamed DRAMBUSTER.

All were given sentences ranging from 15 to 20 years and Lord Grouse of Glenlevit told them as they stood, heads bowed in the dock of the High Court at Edinburgh: "This evil, anti-social and totally selfish type of crime must and will be stamped out.

"No wonder whisky is the price it is with monsters like you fellows on the loose ... cracking open pipes under the sea ... and plundering this precious liquid gold.

"You can count yourselves lucky that Parliament has recently seen fit not to permit the re-introduction of the death penalty otherwise I would be saying to you here and now to prepare for a meeting with your Maker!"

Strong stuff indeed but as a recent opinion poll showed 85% of Scots questioned favoured tough action to crack down on the smugglers.

Some M.P.s have even suggested the setting up of a penal colony on the uninhabited Hebridean island of Gruiniard where the soil is still infected from anthrax used during secret Second World War experiments by the Government.

Another threat to the whisky trade comes in the form of instant whisky which has been developed by the Japanese.

The mere mention of such a revolting concoction makes most Scots want to emigrate to the Moon but it has to be said that the wily Japs are making inroads into the market.

Whisky smuggling is taking on new dimensions since the discovery of wells in the North Sea. Smugglers dive down, drill holes in the pipes and syphon the whisky off.

We can only hope that good taste will prevail.

Certainly there is hope from another recent opinion poll published in one of our major newspapers. Two thousand people from Wick to Coldstream -- a representative cross-section of the population -- were asked if they'd ever tried instant whisky; whether they approved of it in principle; and whether its importation to Britain should be banned.

Only two per cent had tasted it and were unimpressed; seventy nine per cent disapproved of its manufacture; and seventy three per cent called for a complete import ban.

THE PUZZLERS FOLK ASK...

Here are the answers to questions people often ask about whisky.

At what time of the day can a dram be enjoyed most?

Anytime between midnight and midnight.

What should I use as a mixer?

Ideally nothing as the whisky will taste better neat. Water may be added but lemonade is strictly non-U. Would you dance the Slosh naked through the foyer of the Hilton? Answer the call of nature through the window of an express train travelling at 90 miles per hour? Or take your new Catholic girlfriend for a beef curry Friday lunchtime? Of course you wouldn't. Well in the eyes of a true Scotsman putting lemonade in whisky is a much more serious display of anti-social conduct than any of the aforementioned.

How much whisky can I drink without making a fool of myself by losing my memory and falling about the place?

Capacity varies considerably from individual to individual. Generally speaking a quarter bottle leaves the drinker feeling mellow happy and contented.

A half bottle can bring out an aggressive streak if you're still awake. A timid nine-stone man is likely to go home, toss his fat wife's rolling pin into the fire and bash her over the head with a sponge pudding.

Some folk become quite lovey-dovey but such are the ways of nature that a fellow with a half bottle inside his system is often incapable of putting his thoughts into practice.

A full bottle consumed over a pleasant period will do for many what Spinach does for Popeye. At a stroke they'll solve inflation, arrest the threat of a nuclear holocaust and re-create the once mighty British Empire

Trust the Japs — they really are producing powdered whisky! Ugh!

-- "Britain for the British as we used to say in India!" will be the battle-cry of an English aristocrat who downs a bottle.

A full five-giller consumed too quickly will not have the drinker falling about, losing his memory or generally making a fool of himself.

He'll be up in heaven playing his harp!

Can nothing be done about the ridiculous duty slapped on whisky by the Government? I understand it would only cost around £1 a bottle if it wasn't for all the tax.

You are quite correct. But whisky duty is an in-built part of the entire revenue system and brings in millions of pounds a year to the Chancellor of the Exchequer. He makes us pay through the nose in income tax, mortgage repayments etc., knowing full well that we'll go and drown our sorrows in a dram and... hey presto! More lovely loot. If whisky tax were to be cut the state of the economy, believe it or not, would actually be WORSE.

What are some of the more unusual ways of taking whisky?

Well, personally I enjoy a good half pint of whisky and water over my Rice Krispies every morning. It certainly launches me into the day with a snap crackle and pop!

The Irish put tea in their whisky to get Irish tea and we've a neighbour who pours in half a bottle to the pot every time she makes Scotch broth.

But really it's all a question of taste. These are all quite socially acceptable I suppose but, mind you, it's quite amazing what some folk will do with whisky!

Have their been any unusual side-affects from the North Sea exploration for whisky?

Yes -- and we're back to those dreadful smugglers again

Recently three quarters of the population of a north-east fishing village went down with severe alchoholic poisoning...even women and children.

The case was completely baffling as many folk who'd obviously never touched a drop in their lives were affected.

Then enquiries revealed that all the victims had one thing in common--during the previous few days they'd all eaten large amounts of fish.

It transpired that the fish had been swimming in water heavily polluted with whisky after smugglers had fractured a pipe. They were all stoned out of their minds when caught.

A Scotsman's dream — that Campbeltown Loch really was whisky and he could swim it!

As my cousin Jessie McDougall told me later: "We couldn't get over the wonderful taste of the fish and I was eating it morning noon and night".

"Most other folk in the village were the same. They had it for all their meals. Then they started collapsing!"

"The doctors explained that we'd all been eating herring which was 70° proof! No wonder we were ill."

Incidentally I must tell you another funny story about a village being affected by whisky although this wasn't the North Sea variety.

It happened in Argyll a few years ago. A local crofter was out hunting when he spotted a very plump haggis sound asleep in the bushes.

He got out his rifle and fired. But the bullet missed the haggis and went straight into the ground. A few seconds later a brownish thick liquid started spurting from the ground.

Within a minute it had become a fountain shooting fifty feet into the air.

Hopes raised the dumbfounded crofter ran over to see what it was.

Eureka! There was no mistaking the aroma and the taste.

He'd uncovered a whisky well in what was virtually his own back garden.

Word spread through the village like wildfire and folk came rushing from their homes with buckets, jugs, empty bottles... in fact anything that would hold the nippie sweetie!

Our crofter became a multi-millionaire overnight and a few weeks later bought half the shops in Edinburgh's Princes Street which had recently closed down because the operators couldn't afford their rates bills.

Certainly that day in the village will never be forgotten.

It was like the song Campbelltown Loch I wish You Were Whisky coming true on dry land!

Happy islanders strike liquid gold-whisky!

THE CLAN HERDS

The kilt is the Scotsman's delight. In the beginning the Good Lord created the Scots race and a few days later the rest of mankind. The English somehow slipped in the backdoor but their precise origins are lost in the mists of time.

The Scots -- Jock Tamson's bairns -- were seen by God and his heavenly planners as the master race. They would go forth and multiply and these people would travel to all corners of the globe spreading knowledge, beauty, charm and wisdom.

From their number would come the inventors of television... the telephone... wonder drugs like penicillin... the steam engine... even the humble bicycle.

Scotsmen were fashioned by nature to be extra special although surprisingly with all the advantages of modern education and mass communication this is something not generally known outside the shores of our fair kingdom.

It is for this reason that a true Scotsman is at his most comfortable when wearing the kilt. Similarly we have an explanation of why nothing is worn under the kilt.

With the realisation that Scots would be more at ease in a garment other than trousers nature created three breeds of cattle which would give plentiful supplies of the material needed to fashion a loose fitting form of dress.

Over the centuries dozens of new tartans have emerged from the original three through cross breeding.

Twice a year the cows are sheared of their tartan coats and markets are held in many Scottish towns for the sale of the cloth to tailors.

The principal markets are at Oban, Inverness, Perth, Edinburgh and Galashiels.

Clans of course originally grew up around particular breeds of cattle. The biggest herds in those early days belonged to the MacDonalds, Camerons, MacGregors and Campbells. Distinctive colourings from the coats of the cow gave them their particular identity.

The material was first worn as a kind of rough blanket wrapped around the body but in the seventeenth century this gave way to the kilt.

Just like we get wool from sheep.... there are Highland cattle which are sheared for tartan.

THE BOGUS COWS AT BANNOCKBURN

Tartan is a great camouflage in the heather moors and often put Scots at a great advantage during the constant warring with their arch-enemies from the south.

It is not generally known that a brilliant trick involving the clever use of bogus cows helped secure us victory at Bannockburn in 1314.

On the night before the battle a herd of some 500 cattle were moved into meadows next to the English camp. But each cow was really two Scottish soldiers cleverly disguised!

They stood peacefully pretending to chew the grass then when the English and Scots were in full battle they threw off their disguise... and attacked the Sassenachs from the rear!

The cow also provides another vital necessity... the sporran. These are hatched from eggs which are laid three times a year --on April 1, August Bank Holiday Monday and Hogmanay -- and it is not unknown to have as many as five sporrans in one egg.

The sporran is a cheeky wee chap with a pouch just like a kangaroo. This makes him ideal as the 'pocket' of the kilt.

Sporrans never grow beyond a few inches on account of the fact that their staple diet is condensed milk and shortbread.

It should be said that Scottish cows, unlike the English variety don't give milk.

They produce wee heavy beer instead and every morning tankers arrive at farms to collect the magic brew and disperse it to hostelries throughout the kingdom.

Only snag is that some cowmaids like the stuff so much they keep drinking it before breakfast and end up tipsy.

Just recently the House of Commons Scottish Grand Committee agreed to set up a special inquiry into the problem of drunkenness among these women.

One breed of Highland cows doesn't give milk — they give beer instead! No wonder the cowgirl is merry!

The Lesser Known Flora & Fauna of Scotland

THE MONKS WHO DISCOVERED PORRIDGE

Some people think that porridge comes from a plant called the oat which grows to around three feet in height.

Obviously they've never heard of the porridge mines which employ thousands of men and women in Lanarkshire, Ayrshire and the Lothians.

But let us begin at the beginning.

Porridge was first discovered on these shores seven centuries ago by monks at Newbattle Abbey in Midlothian.

One morning two of the brothers, John and Mark, were out for a stroll along the River Esk.

Suddenly the sky became dull and overcast and it started to rain.

Rather than run the risk of getting soaked to the skin by heading back to the monastery the two took shelter in a little cave by the waterside.

Whilst waiting for the rain to subside Brother John looked up at the roof of the cave and chanced to see a jelly-like layer protruding from the stonework.

"How intriguing -- what can that be?" he asked his companion.

"I don't know. But I'll give you a leg up to have a closer look," replied Mark.

John scooped some of the stuff off with a knife and carefully wrapped it in a cloth.

They then made their way back to the monastery where the find was presented to the wise old abbot.

Never one to dilly dally the abbot cut off a small piece and popped it in his mouth.

"Delicious! Simply delicious!" he cried.

"Brothers you have stumbled on a wonderful delicacy." Next day at dawn the abbot and several of the monks went with John and Mark to the cave.

Closer inspection revealed a huge gap in the side of the roof which led into a maze of caverns. The walls were all thickly lined with the tasty substance which was subsequently named porridge.

At the porridge face down the mine!

The name comes from ancient Midlothianese ... pairradgee or food of the Lord.

Never slow to miss the opportunity of making a fast shilling or two -- after all they had discovered coal near the same spot a few years previously -- the monks set up an operation to 'harvest' the pairradgee.

It was then washed in the cool waters of the River Esk cut into slices and hung out to dry on the tall pine trees which then graced the valley of the Esk in such great abundance.

Soon this new food became one of the best selling lines at markets in Haddington, Dalkeith, Peebles, Penicuik and Musselburgh.

THE LORD AND THE DEVIL WORK TOGETHER

Oddly enough it was a local witch called Camp Meg who first had the idea of adding milk and salt to a plateful of the pairradgee -- a unique case surely of the Lord and the Devil combining to start something which would revolutionise the eating habits of all Scots!

The rest of course is history.

With the coming of the industrial revolution man sank shafts into the ground and dug more deeply in his quest for porridge. railways meant that porridge could be transported quickly and cheaply from the minehead to shops all over the country.

In fishing towns husbands go to sea and bring home the catch for their wives to gut and clean.

With porridge things are much the same.

A miner at the porridge face -- who can now earn as much as £250 a week before tax -- works with efficient clean modern machinery to produce the porridge slices.

On the surface women are employed to wash the porridge and cut it into slices for despatch.

Traditionally the porridge is bought in five layer packs by the housewife and kept in a bottom drawer in the kitchenette.

Porridge girls cut up the goodies!

Each morning they can cut off a portion for dividing up amongst the family.

In my view this is certainly a much better practice than the all-too common convenience method of nowadays. Sadly two out of every five Scots now prefer to buy imitation porridge.

This comes in a packet containing flakey stuff. As I understand it you simply add water and bring to the boil stirring all the time.

And they say we're a civilised nation!

THE SHY BAGPIPE TREE

Deep in the heart of many Scottish pine forests lies one of nature's most timid and wonderful creations --the bagpipe tree.

Few ordinary people, even in Scotland, are fortunate enough to see the trees in bloom because they grow in only the remotest spots.

And, sadly, the bagpipe tree only plays its merry tune for one hour a year. So someone who can find a tree and be there at the right time for the music is fortunate indeed.

The trees bloom in spring just once every five years with the sprouting of the chanter followed a few weeks later by the rest of the instrument and the gradual expansion of the bag.

They can thrive only in the Scottish climate and attempts to re-plant in the United States, Canada, and Australia have proved disastrous.

Similarly an attempt to cash in on the tourist trade by uprooting trees from the Perthshire hills and installing them in Princes Street Gardens, Edinburgh, flopped when the bagpipes shrivelled up and died.

Soon after this outrage the B.T.P.A. -- Bagpipe Tree Protection Association -- was formed to spare us from further transplants and today it numbers some of the most eminent people in the kingdom amongst its members.

In the ancient forests of Caledonia the bagpipe trees flourished in their tens of thousands and at harvest time there were plenty of instruments for all the natives.

But over the past few centuries the number of trees has shrunk drastically and Parliament has introduced special protection orders which makes the removal of instruments from the trees or damage to

The singing bagpipe tree.

the roots or branches punishable by up to five years imprisonment.

This short supply has led to the creation of firms which specialise in man-made bagpipes. Such is the wonderful skill of the craftsmen involved that these instruments look and sound perfectly natural.

And recently this has been taken a step further by the development of electronic pipes which means that players can forget about huffing and puffing and concentrate on the playing.

But for me there is nothing to beat the real McCoy I am fortunate to be the proud owner of an instrument handed down from my great-grandfather and it still has many years of life left yet as the average bagpipe can survive for up to 300 years.

And their diet of oatcakes is certainly much cheaper than electricity!

AMERICANS IN CALEDONIA

Recently I asked some of our American cousins on holiday here how they were enjoying their vacation in bonnie Scotland.

Here are a few typical comments received.

"Gee I jus' think your little ol' country is wonderful -- we were sailin' today on a great little pond with miniature bridges over it. I think you call it the Forth or somethin'" -- Oilman from Texas.

"Edinburgh is sure beautiful honey. Your town planners are much more thoughtful than back in the States -- I mean the way you've built the castle so close to the Rail Station in Edinburgh. That's good thinking.

"By the way we are thinking of going over to Ayrshire to see Bobbie Burns. Do you know if he'll be at home today?" -- mother of five from Kentucky.

"Great! Fantastic! Marvellous! We've been here since last night after coming up from London. We'll take in all the Scotch sites before doing Paris tomorrow and the other main capitals before the week-end." --couple from New York.

"Hey, most of you Scotch guys aren't very tall. I asked a kid at our hotel about that and he said its because you're all brought up on shortbread and condensed milk. I though it was a gag at first until the manager explained to me that its a Scotch tradition for

Some folk are not content to leave things to nature — there is now such a thing as an artificial bagpipe!

anyone over six feet to buy the first round of drinks" -- midget from Memphis.

"You're leaders are much better than Nixon or Reagan and co. If we'd Bobby the Bruce or Sir Bill Wallace in the White House I'm sure the Kremlin would take us more seriously" -- schoolteacher from Kansas.

"Good ol' Scotch whisky sure takes some beatin'. Especially in porridge. The combination has made me superfit since the start of my vacation four days ago.

"It'll be real super when they finish the Scott Monument in Princes Street. I climbed it the other day and it was just like being on the third floor of the Empire State Building" -- Government worker from Washington.

"Scenery is pretty good although not as dramatic as in some parts of the States. I mean you've no real rivers, mountains or lakes. Still we've got some not bad snaps of the Grampian foothills, the Spey stream and a pond at Luss -- is it Lomond?

"Have a nice day" -- movie star from Hollywood.
YOU'RE WELCOME!

GEEZABREK!

The Scots, it is said, are wary of strangers or giving anything away for nothing.

Even a simple question like, "How are you?" is likely to meet with the immediate response, "Hoo's yersel?" and absolutely no information as to the native's state of health wealth or whatever.

This in-bred suspicious approach to life does not always do the sons and daughters of Caledonia well.

A story is told of the Perthshire villagers who idled away their lives refusing to work, chasing women and drinking hard.

The parish minister constantly warned his wayward flock that their conduct would bar them from entering the gates of heaven but his advice fell on deaf ears.

The only spirit world that interested them was the gantry behind the bar.

But all bad -- or good things depending on your outlook -- must come to an end and one Hogmanay a light plane crashed through the pub roof. The regulars were killed instantly.

A few moments later they found themselves surrounded by the burning fires of hell.

They began praying for all their worth and a vision of their minister, who had departed for heaven just two weeks previously, appeared before them.

"Meenister, meenister, tak us oot o' this place", they cried.

"We didna ken. We didna ken. We repent all our past folly.

"Meenister we didna ken!"

There was a short pause -- expectancy filled the hot air. Would they be forgiven?

But after what seemed an age the minister bellowed back: "Well, ye ken noo!" and evaporated into eternity.

This reminds me -- although don't ask how -- of the 72 year old resident in a Glasgow eventide home who fell in love with and wanted to marry a girl of 19.

Tongues started to wag and fellow staff and residents were against the proposed match.

So the would-be groom turned to his 93-year-old father for advice.

"What should I do dad. Is the age gap of 53 years too much?"

The dad lingered over a few puffs from his pipe and then with a twinkle in his eye, replied: "Laddie... ye'll ken yir ain business best."

Natives of course have a powerful weapon when it comes to baffling the English and other visitors ... their local dialects.

On the surface it would seem fair to assume that a tourist from, say London, would be able to make himself understood in a Glasgow city centre pub.

Let's set the scene.

He walks up to the bar and says: "I say old chap...a half please!

The day is hot and he is looking forward to a refreshing beer.

A moment or two later a whisky is thrust before him and the barman says: "Pony'strotter is owererr in rajug orrifya fancy Harvey'sblade that'll be another twintypee".

(Which quickly translated means that water was availabe in a nearby jug: a dash of lemonade would involve expenditure of a further twenty pence.)

The tourist however was angry and said: "But my man. I asked for a half. A half you fool. And in England that means a half pint of beer. Take this back instantly".

"Ach awa and bile yir heid ye daft eejit ye -- yir in Glesca no poncy bloody London. Geezabrek ye wee Bengallancer ye."

(Quick translation: Kindly desist from criticism. By Glasgow custom you have been served the correct measure. Please allow me to get on with my job and I have to say that I have you marked down as something of a chancer).

The tourist grew quite red in the face and demanded to see the manager.

"He's awa furraferr wi rawifeanweansanat -- ah'm in charge ya nyaff anadsoonerstoatyeaffrawa than chingeyirbevvy."

(Translation: The manager is on vacation with his wife, children and in-laws for the local summer break. I'm in charge and I feel that I can be of little further constructive assistance to you.)

More exchanges followed but to cut a long story short the tourist was forced to down his whisky and venture out into the night as loser of the argument.

SEE YOU JIST NOW

Dialects vary quite considerably around the country.

Consider a situation where a perfectly law abiding citizen has adjourned after an evening supping jars of ale with his chums in the local hostelry and is returning to his beloved wife.

The call of nature sounds midway between tavern and home and the village public loo is closed. He decides to relieve himself... completely unaware that two dedicated members of Her Majesty's constabulary are a few paces behind.

Caught red-handed so to speak he is charged with committing a nuisance...

In such circumstances the Glaswegian is likely to reply: "Oh ma Goad! Hae yooseyins nuthin' better tae dae wi yir time. Geezabrek an'droap the chairge."

(Translation: I'm sure you kind sires have other more pressing matters to deal with. Please let me go.)

In Midlothian the response would be: "Adorsitychrist! Ah suppose ah'm the best ye can dae ... an' murderers and rapists on the loose a' ower the place."

(Translation: I dare say to Christ that a case like this must test your full knowledge in the laws of detection. And all this with dangerous people like killers on the loose.)

In Aberdeen we could expect: "Fit, ma loons. Quick, turn roon. Fa's tat quine be'an attacked doon the road there?"

Quick translation: "What-ho my boys! Quick, glance to your rear! Who is that girl being attacked further down the street." There is of course no attack but when police attention is diverted the Aberdonian makes a quick getaway.

The Dundonian faced with such circumstances might reply: "Help ma' boab! Em telling ye em no gonna tak this leein' doon."

(Translation: Golly gosh! We'll see what the chief constable has to say about this!)

Yes, dialects are funny.

In Caithness when folk part -- even if they're not going to be together again for weeks -- the farewell comment is usually "See you jist now!"

In an Aberdeenshire town the Queen could be lunching with the district council chairman at a local hotel and some worthy would no doubt pose the question: Fa's tat wae tha provost?

When neighbours meet in the Western Isles the immortal question is posed: "Tonald! Is it yourself?"

Whether its expected that Tonald, or Morag or Seamus or whoever may have been taken over by some demon and tis better to double check first... well I'm not entirely sure.

And all this gives me absolutely no reason whatever to slip in that immortal little rhyme by way of conclusion to this chapter:-

Here's tae us! Wha's like us?

Damn few!

An' they're deid!

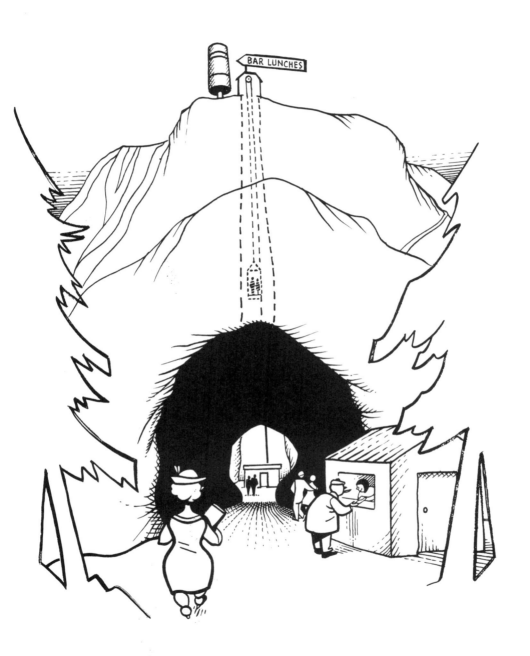

A drink in the restaurant on top of Ben Nevis is quite an experience!

A CONDENSED TALE

Another little known peculiarity of Scotland's story is that we gave the world condensed milk.

Now produced artificially condensed milk was the staple diet of natives who lived in the heart of the Trossachs centuries ago.

Because of the rough thick woodland and lack of proper communication with the outside world -- no roads for example -- Troschanians were unable to keep traditional farm animals to provide them with the essentials for a staple diet.

They had to rely on catching the occasional stag and on the minmac.

The minmac was a kind of miniature cow, sadly now almost extinct, which grew to eight pounds maximum weight and had four tiny udders.

Each minmac was capable -- we say was because none have been seen in the past 10 years and experts put their numbers now at no more than a conservative 80 -- of producing six pints of condensed milk a day.

An individual family of Troschanians would keep a herd of 50 or so minmacs and their surplus milk was sold at the market in Callander or exchanged for other goods like flour.

To transport the milk through the thick woodland Troschanians employed the aid of the little faery folk who on account of only being a foot tall were much more nimble of foot and delivered the milk to humans living on the edge of the forest who made the rest of the commercial arrangements.

Trouble with the little folk was that over the centuries they became more and more greedy demanding ridiculously large amounts for transporting the milk.

Eventually the humans were forced to move from their woodland hideaways and find sustenance in the more open lands of Argyll.

Abandoned and unmilked the poor minmacs just grew and grew until they burst.

Those that survive today do so only because the faery folk milk them for their own domestic needs.

But such are the wonders of science that chemists have devised a way of producing condensed milk in tins fit for human consumption.

NOW TO BE SERIOUS...

I hope that you have enjoyed our journey through Scotland. Is truth stranger than fiction?

We conclude this tour with a quick look at some real-life news stories which have appeared in the newspapers over the past few years connected with whisky, porridge, tartan, haggis and all that...

In 1975 Superstar the bull was causing a major headache at a Haddington farm. He just wasn't interested in the 22 heifers!

Various love cures were tried without success.

Then along came a piper and the magic sound of the bagpipes did the trick.

After hearing the drone of our national instrument Superstar was spurred to greater things.

It was later reported: All 22 heifers are in calf.

YOUR UDDER NATIONAL DRINK...

ITS YOUR UDDER NATIONAL DRINK ran the headline on the story which revealed that workers in a scientific laboratory had discovered how to get whisky from a cow.

The chemist who headed the research team said that the average cow gives about 1,250 gallons of milk a year. This is enough to produce 50 gallons of alcohol.

His Dutch lab was refining whey ... the substance left over when milk is turned into cheese.

Some Scotsmen are mean when it comes to serving up a dram!

ODD BUT TRUE

A row blew up when the Australian Government concluded that sporrans were luxuries ... and imposed a £25 import duty on them.

Furious pipe bandsmen across the country pointed out that the sporran was essential for keeping odds and ends in.

After all kilts have no pockets!

A sustained pressure campaign forced the Government to relent in April, 1976.

From that date sporrans could be imported tax free ... officially recognised as an essential part of the national dress.

Haggis hurling championships became a new national sport in 1976.

Oddly enough the idea was thought up by an IRISHMAN around the time of the Gathering of the Clans.

Huge crowds turned out to watch this new form of entertainment and before long an official world Haggis Hurling Association was born.

Branches were formed in America, Australia and Canada.

Like all records new competitors come along to change them but at the time of writing the champion hurler is a fellow who threw a one and a half pounder 158 feet five inches.

Problems are caused by haggis which burst when they come back down to earth.

So dogs have now been trained as retrievers to save the country being littered with remains of that great chieftain o' the puddin' race!

An exiled Scot in Wisconsin, U.S.A., had two toes amputated so that he could keep on playing the bagpipes.

They were transplanted on to his right hand to replace two fingers lost in an accident.

The operation in a Kentucky hospital took more than 11 hours.

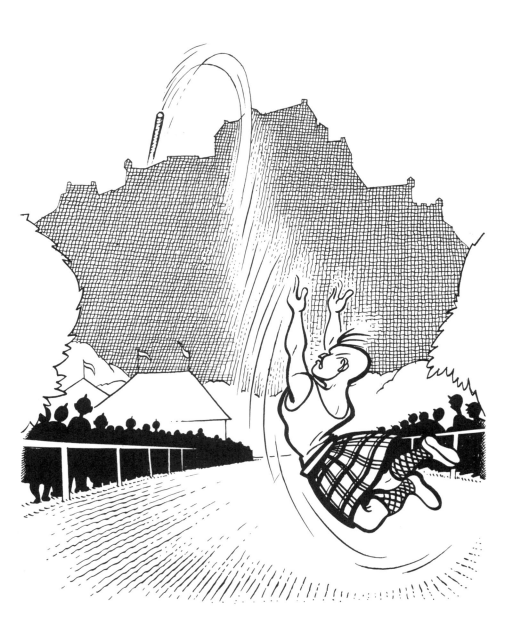

The strongest Scotsman Hamish MacMuckle tosses the caber over Edinburgh Castle to land at Portobello.

CHAMP HAGGIS GUZZLERS

The world's champion haggis eater at the time of writing has retained his title for the fourth year in a row by scoffing a one and a half pounder in just one minute 51 seconds.

The young Scot was 30 seconds faster than his runner-up and saw off rivals from England, France, Germany and the U.S.A.

Being an enthusiastic bagpipe player can have its problems

Magistrates at Brighton heard the case of a company director who hired a church hall to practice in.

A neighbour was so angered by the din that he kicked the door in and broke the hinge.

The court was told that the piper had just laughed when the accused asked him to stop playing.

Still, piping on private premises is legal. Kicking in doors isn't.

The neighbour was fined £20.

In another case a piper ended up in the dock. This time at Glasgow.

He'd been playing Scotland the Brave all day in the street and ignored requests to move on.

A sympathetic magistrate imposed an admonition but warned: "sometimes bagpipe playing can be annoying..."

A piper's lament fell on deaf ears at a London court in 1979. He was found guilty by Thames magistrates of obstructing the highway at the Tower of London.

The player claimed in court that entertainers were given free access to the area under a charter granted by King George III in 1797.

If he was guilty of obstruction then so was the governor of the Tower for allowing queues of a thousand or more to form on the pavement.

The magistrates however were unimpressed and imposed a fine of £10.

In that same year the citizens of William Shakespeare's home town of Stratford-on-Avon silenced the bagpipes.

APRIL 1, 1981. After being captured in Loch Ness the monster affectionately known as Nessie was taken in a special train to Edinburgh. Here she is being marched along Princes Street to a new aquarium.

Two pipers had been hired to play outside Scottish wool shops for six hours a day as part of an effort to attract customers.

But for locals it was all a huge turn-off.

After a string of complaints over three weeks the health department of the council searched through old records and produced an ancient bye-law which had been made to curb the activities of strolling players.

In September, 1977, the song Campbeltown Loch I Wish You Were Whisky took on something of a new twist.

Bang on opening time at 11 a.m. nearly three thousand gallons of the cratur flowed into Loch Lomond when an articulated lorry shed its valuable load after a valve on the tanker burst open.

KILT WAS THEIR DELIGHT...

Lucky passengers on helicopter flights between London's Heathrow and Gatwick Airports discovered the secret of what's worn under the kilt.

As the choppers went up and down so did tartan skirts worn by stewardess staff.

The blast of air from the rotor arms gave their skirts a Highland fling over their heads!

To spare further blushes airline bosses stepped in and prescribed a skirt with fewer pleats which fits tighter than the usual kilt ... and green underskirts heavy enough to defeat the strongest gusts!

In 1976 scientists reported that Army kilts can have more than 100 shades of the main colours all requiring different threads.

So they proposed -- as an economy measure -- that the number of shades be slashed to three green, three blues, two reds and an ordinary black and white.

Put an old kilt beside a new one and nobody will know the difference decreed the boffins.

But this economy measure brought a sharp response from at least one newspaper leader column headlined: "Wha daur meddle wi' me?" And the writer asked: "Is somebody looking for another Bannockburn?"

The wee folk in Scotland get up to a lot of mischief.

The biggest haggis in the world, at the time of writing, weighed in at 24 stones six pounds beating the previous record by fourteen pounds.

Displayed in a Glasgow butcher's shop it took a day to make, measured three feet by two feet and needed two men to carry it.

Later the haggis was taken apart for distribution among old folk and charities.

A haggis firm's sales doubled in a fortnight after husbands claimed that a plateful had made their previously childless wives pregnant.

But tests carried out by scientists in 1969 proved that the women's conditions must have been due to something else!

For there was nothing in the haggis to make it a source of fertility.

BIG DADDY'S BAN

Big Daddy Idi Amin of Uganda caused a major headache for bagpipe manufacturers in 1974 when he imposed a ban on the export of African blackwood from his country.

Bagpipe makers had relied on it for years to produce their chanters and drones.

In 1978 a half of whisky offended the oil rich sheiks of Saudi Arabia ... even though it was only a picture on a can of haggis!

Hundreds of exiled Scots workers had to do without their beloved pudding on Burns night after officials refused to allow the cans into the strictly no-alcohol country.

A survey published in April, 1981, disclosed that Scots appeared to have forsaken whisky as their national drink.

Sixty seven per cent of Scots questioned in a survey of two thousand people said that they never touched the cratur.

Others -- horror of horror -- admitted that they added lemonade and not the traditional water to their drams.

Thirty two per cent of Scots liked vodka compared with the national average of 20 per cent.

But bagpipe players presumably still enjoy a dram. A factory manufacturing wood and baize bagpipe cases in the North incorporates sections for the chanter, drones, spare parts, music ... and a half bottle of whisky.

In 1978 electronic bagpipes were developed in Paisley. They sound just like the real thing. Because they don't need to be blown players can concentrate one hundred per cent on the music.

Later that same year the Japanese announced that they had perfected powdered whisky.

Plugging in to play the pipes and pouring powder from a sachet into a glass of water for a dram?

Rabbie Burns will be birling in his grave!

Sporrans hatch from their eggs.